BLAZE AND THE FOREST FIRE

BLAZE AND THE FOREST FIRE

BY C. W. ANDERSON

 HOUGHTON MIFFLIN   BOSTON • MORRIS PLAINS, NJ

California   •   Colorado   •   Georgia   •   Illinois   •   New Jersey   •   Texas

By C. W. Anderson

Billy and Blaze

Blaze and the Forest Fire

Blaze and the Mountain Lion

Blaze and Thunderbolt

Blaze Finds the Trail

Blaze and the Indian Cave

Blaze and the Lost Quarry

Blaze and the Gray Spotted Pony

Blaze Shows the Way

Blaze and the
Forest Fire

Billy was a boy who loved horses more than anything else in the world. He loved his own pony, Blaze, best of all. After his father and mother gave him Blaze, Billy spent most of his time with the pony. Blaze would come whenever Billy called. He seemed to like the rides through the woods or along the roads as much as Billy did. Billy felt sure that Blaze understood him when he talked; and the pony really did seem to understand what Billy said.

Billy's dog, Rex, usually went with them on their rides. But one day he was sick; so Billy's mother kept him at home. It was a beautiful day, and Billy decided to ride along a little winding road. It passed through some woods, and not many people used it. Both Billy and Blaze liked to ride through the woods, because there were so many things to see. They always met rabbits and squirrels and saw many birds. Flowers grew along the way, and the big trees were green and cool after the hot, dusty roads. The summer had been very warm, and there had been little rain.

2

They had gone quite a long way when Blaze suddenly stopped. Billy looked ahead and saw smoke coming out of a pile of dry brush at the side of the road. He knew that it was against the law to build fires in the woods during the dry season. It was not a safe thing to do because of the danger of starting a forest fire.

Even as Billy looked, the flames burst
out. He knew that these flames were
the beginning of a forest fire unless they
could be put out. If a breeze came up
and carried the fire to the big pine trees
nearby, the whole countryside might
burn. Not only the grass and trees
would be burned. Fences and barns and
houses would also go up in flames.

Billy had once seen a place where a forest fire had been. He remembered how bare and black it had looked, with burned stumps where beautiful trees had been. He knew he must try to save the woods he loved so much. He must go quickly and get help.

The nearest place to go for help was a large farm. It was a long way to this farm by the road, and there was no time to lose. Billy knew they could save much time if they cut across country through the fields. But to reach the first field they would have to jump a high stone wall, higher than anything Blaze had ever jumped. But Blaze seemed to understand that they needed to hurry. He jumped the high wall perfectly.

Then they went on as fast as they could across the wide field. Billy did not need to urge Blaze. The pony was going like the wind. If he could only keep up this speed, they would soon reach the farmhouse. Billy could see it far off in the distance.

In the middle of the field was a brook. There was no bridge and no time to look for a shallow place to cross. "Come on, Blaze," called Billy, and Blaze went even faster than before. The nearer they came to the brook, the wider it seemed. It was too late to stop now. They were right at the water's edge.

Blaze made a tremendous leap. Billy could feel how hard he was trying. It seemed that they would surely get over the brook safely.

As they landed, the bank gave way
under the pony's hind feet. For a
moment Billy thought they would fall
back into the brook. But Blaze scrambled
up the bank, and Billy held on somehow,
his arms around the pony's neck.

In a flash Billy had his feet in the stirrups again; and they were off as fast as the faithful pony could go. Blaze was breathing hard now, but the farmhouse was near.

Suddenly Billy pulled Blaze to a stop. There, right in front of them, was a high wall with barbed wire at the top. He looked both ways but there was no gate in sight. Billy almost gave up, but the thought of the fire sweeping across the countryside was too much. They must go on.

"Just once more, Blaze," he whispered to the pony. Poor Blaze was very tired, but he galloped bravely toward the fence. He was straining every muscle for the jump.

They were almost over when Billy felt Blaze's hind legs catch on the wire, and they began to fall.

Down went Blaze to his knees, and
Billy slipped out of the saddle and up
on the pony's neck. It seemed certain
that Blaze would go down all the way,
taking Billy with him.

But, with a great effort, Blaze scrambled to his feet; and Billy, holding on to the pony's neck, stayed on. Then Blaze started at a gallop for the farmhouse, which was just across the field.

They galloped into the farmyard. The farmer and his son hurried over to meet Billy. All out of breath, he told them about the fire. At once they got some things to use in putting it out. Then they climbed into a car and drove off very fast. The farmer's wife quickly telephoned to the neighbors to send all the help they could.

Blaze was covered with sweat and dirt. He was a very tired pony, but he rubbed his nose against Billy and seemed to know that the boy was proud of him.

"You're the best pony in the world, Blaze —the very best!" said Billy, and he felt sure that what he said was true.

The barbed wire had cut Blaze's legs.
So the farmer's wife brought warm
water and medicine and helped Billy
wash the cuts clean and bandage them.
They were not deep cuts, and the
farmer's wife said she was sure they
would soon heal.

Billy and Blaze had a good rest at the
farmhouse and something to eat. Then
Billy started for home, letting Blaze
walk slowly. On the way they met the
farmers coming back. They said that
they had been able to put out the fire
before it did any real harm. They all
thanked Billy for what he had done.
They made him feel quite grown up.
They said nice things about Blaze too;
so Billy was very happy as he rode
home.

When Billy got home, his father and mother were waiting for him. The farmer's wife had telephoned to tell them what had happened. Billy's father took some salve and put it on Blaze's cuts so that they would heal more quickly. Blaze got much petting, and had some carrots with his supper. He was very fond of carrots. Billy had some chocolate cake with his supper. He liked that just as much as Blaze liked carrots. Billy's father and mother were very proud of both Billy and Blaze.

One evening, two weeks later, there was a rap at the door. Billy's mother asked him to go and see who was there. It was one of the farmers who had helped put out the fire. He held a big box on which was written FOR BILLY AND BLAZE.

Much excited, Billy opened the box. He found a beautiful new bridle, with a silver headband on which was printed one word—BLAZE. The box held also a pair of shiny new boots and a fine pair of riding breeches. They were just the right size for Billy. The people of the countryside had bought all these things for him. They wanted to show Billy how grateful they were that he had saved them from a forest fire.

It was hard to sleep that night. It seemed to Billy that daylight would never come. He got up several times to look at the new boots and the beautiful bridle. He wanted to be sure he hadn't dreamed them.

No one else was awake when Billy
brought the new bridle down to the
stable and put it on Blaze. Even Rex
was still asleep. When Billy got into the
saddle wearing his new breeches and
boots, he felt fine. He was sure he
could ride better because he had them
on. Blaze arched his neck proudly. Even
in the early dawn the silver headband
on the new bridle shone brightly. His
cuts were all healed; and he felt fine,
too. So the two friends started happily
off for their early-morning ride.